NEW ENGLAND

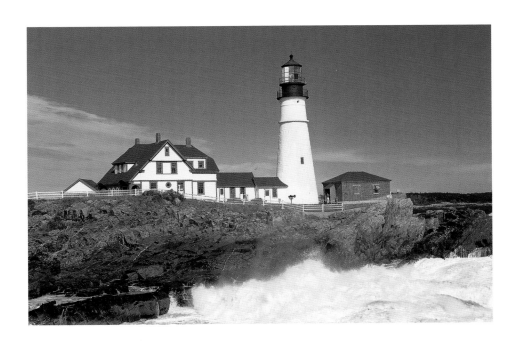

whitecap

The information in this book is true and complete to the best of the author's knowledge. All recommendations are made
without guarantee on the part of the author or Whitecap Books Ltd. The author and publisher disclaim any liability in
connection with the use of this information. For additional information please contact Whitecap Books Ltd.,
at 351 Lynn Avenue, North Vancouver, British Columbia, Canada V7J 2C4.

Edited by Lisa Collins
Proofread by Elizabeth McLean
Text and photo editing by Tanya Lloyd Kyi
Cover and interior design by Steve Penner
Typeset by Tanya Lloyd Kyi
Front cover photograph by W. Cody/First Light
Back cover photograph by Tom Till

Printed and bound in China

Library and Archives Canada Cataloguing in Publication

Lloyd, Tanya, 1973–
    New England

    ISBN 1-55110-947-6 (hardcover) — ISBN 1-55285-790-5 (paperback)
    ISBN 978-1-55110-947-3 (hardcover) — ISBN 1-55285-790-8 (paperback)

    1. New England—Pictorial works. I. Title.

F5.L54 199966   1998974'.043'022266   1998C99-910830-1

The publisher acknowledges the financial support of the Government of Canada through the Canada Book Fund (CBF)
and the province of British Columbia through the Book Publishing Tax Credit

For more information on the America series and other Whitecap Books titles, please visit our website at www.whitecap.ca.

Wander down a lane in Vermont or stroll through one of Maine's coastal villages and you could easily find yourself swept back a century in time. The history that seemed staid and boring in your high school textbooks suddenly springs to life, complete with daring heroes, traitorous villains, rebellions, and revolutions. A visitor to Plymouth, for example, might find Pilgrims firing their muskets. A traveler in Providence might see the church of Roger Williams, who founded the Baptist denomination here after the Puritans banished him for his "dangerous" ideas.

And if it feels like you're walking in the footsteps of Mark Twain as you explore Connecticut's streets, you could be. Both Twain and Harriet Beecher Stowe, author of *Uncle Tom's Cabin,* were once residents of Hartford. Literature and art lovers can peek into Thoreau's cabin on Walden Pond, view Archibald M. Willard's famous painting *The Spirit of '76* in Marblehead, or stop at the House of Seven Gables, which inspired Nathaniel Hawthorne.

If you're more interested in the attractions of today than those of yesterday, enjoy the Faneuil Hall Marketplace in Boston, ski the steep slopes of Mount Mansfield, or celebrate the Pumpkin Festival with the thousands of revelers in Keene. You can stroll the trails of Acadia National Park, sail across the pale, early morning waters of Lake Champlain, or let a gondola sweep you to the summit of Mount Washington.

But as you enjoy these sights, keep in mind that behind the lighthouses, harbors, and maple trees that tempt so many people to tour New England each year, there lies a rich and varied past. Soon, you may find yourself speaking of characters such as Paul Revere, Alexander Graham Bell, and Elihu Yale as if you were once the best of friends.

Acadia National Park
encompasses 35,000
acres, ranging from
rocky seashores to
mountain passes.
The preserve was
founded in 1913,
when President
Wilson set aside
6,000 acres. More
than one million
people now visit
the park each year.

Most commercial fishers have traded their old lobster traps for wire ones. The wooden traps have become sought-after souvenirs of Maine's coast.

More than 120 miles of hiking trails allow visitors to explore the rugged terrain of Acadia National Park. Carriage roads, closed to vehicle traffic, also grant backcountry access to mountain bikers.

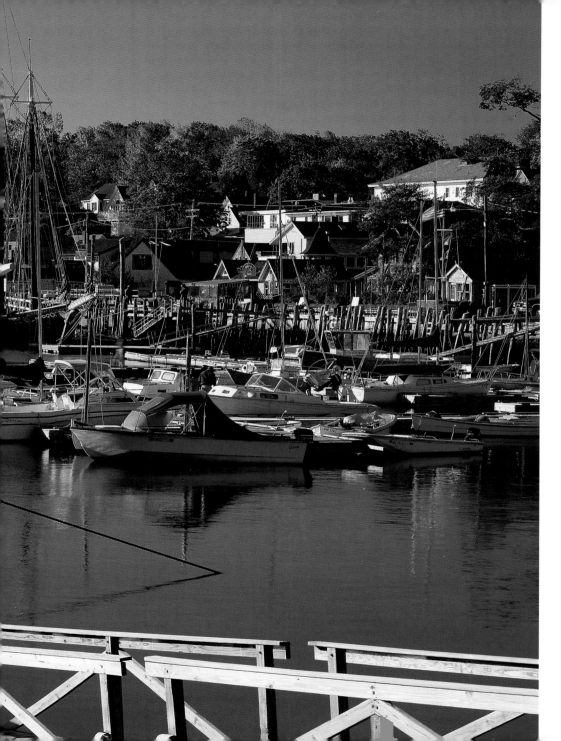

A wooden walkway leads to the *Mary Day*, docked in Camden's harbor. While the town's shops and inns draw thousands of tourists, the harbor is a familiar port to sailors all along the Atlantic coast.

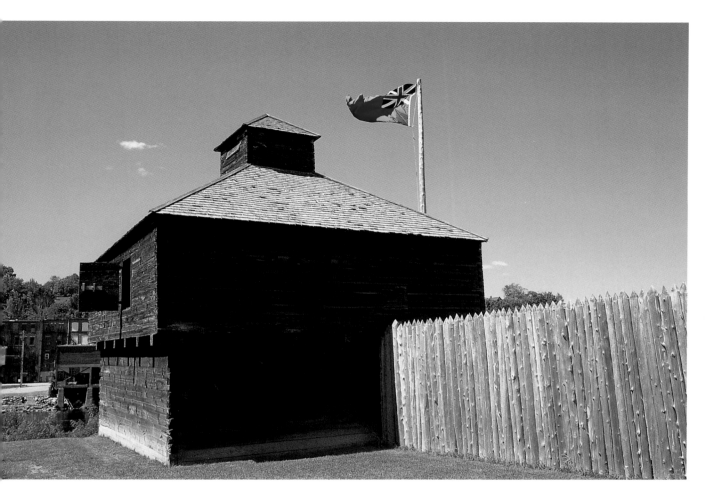

The oldest wooden fort in New England, Fort Western was built in 1754. The bastion was an essential defense post on the Kennebec River and a launching point for Benedict Arnold's forces during the American Revolution.

Augusta is both the capital of Maine and the seat of Kennebec County. More than 20,000 people live in the city, which spreads along the banks of the Kennebec River.

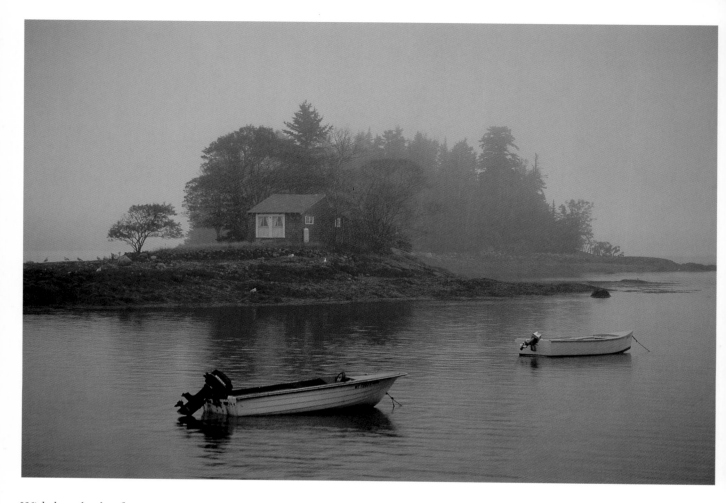

With hundreds of coves, promontories, and offshore
islands, the Maine coast is an astounding 3,478 miles long.

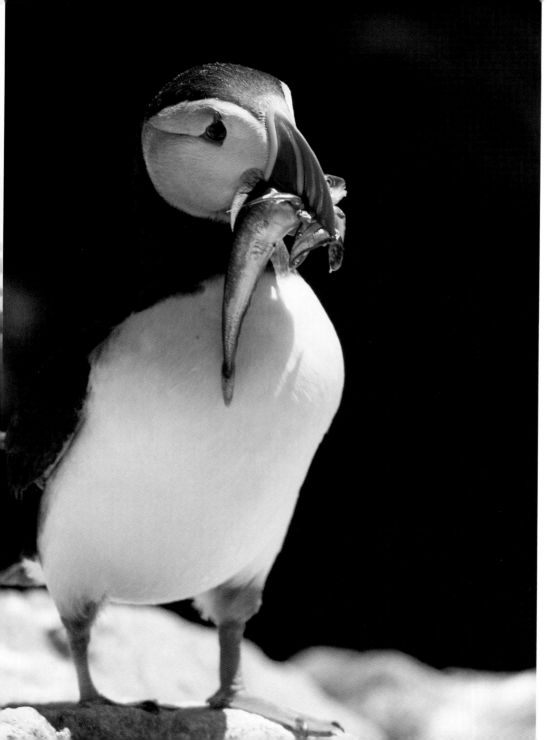

Lined with hooks, the puffin's bill is uniquely suited to scooping up herring. These birds have been known to carry up to 60 small fish at once.

15

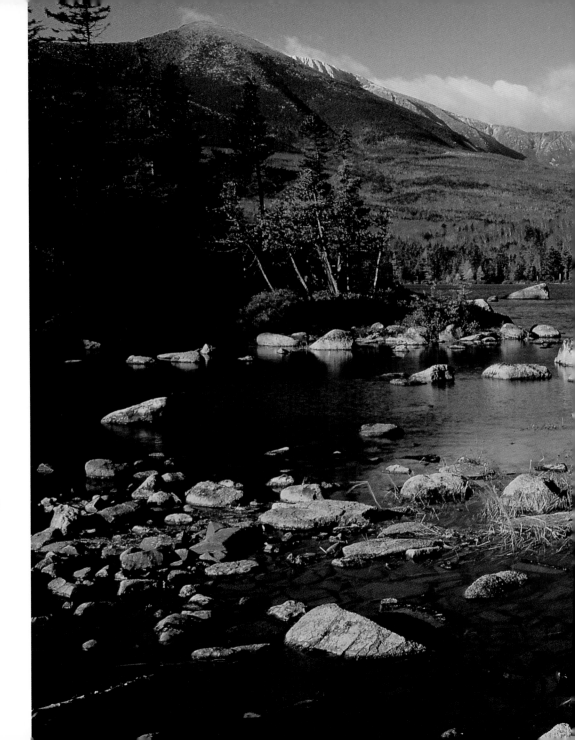

A favorite destination for campers, hikers, and rock climbers, 205,000-acre Baxter State Park was a gift to Maine from Governor Percival Baxter, who bought the land in 1931.

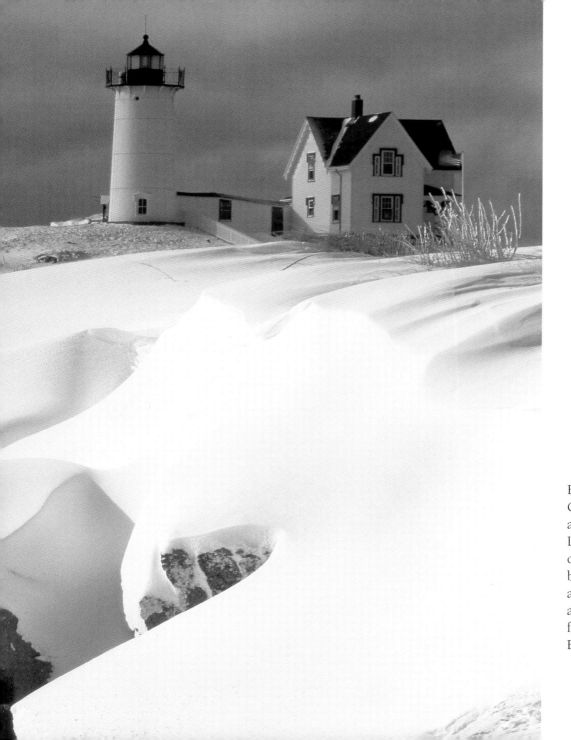

Established in 1879, Cape Neddick Light — also known as Nubble Light for its position on a rocky "nub- ble" — stands next to a clapboard house and white picket fence typical of New England's beacons.

This blooming blue flag is one of more than 2,000 flowering plants and ferns that thrive in mountain meadows and under the canopy of New England's forests.

The winds that sweep the summit of New Hampshire's Mount Washington can reach over 200 miles per hour. The peak is part of White Mountain National Forest, the largest expanse of public land in New England.

The deluxe Mount Washington Hotel and Resort opened its doors in 1902 and has been a New Hampshire landmark ever since. Visitors can enjoy the mountain air from the 900-foot-long verandah or tour the lush grounds in a horse-drawn carriage.

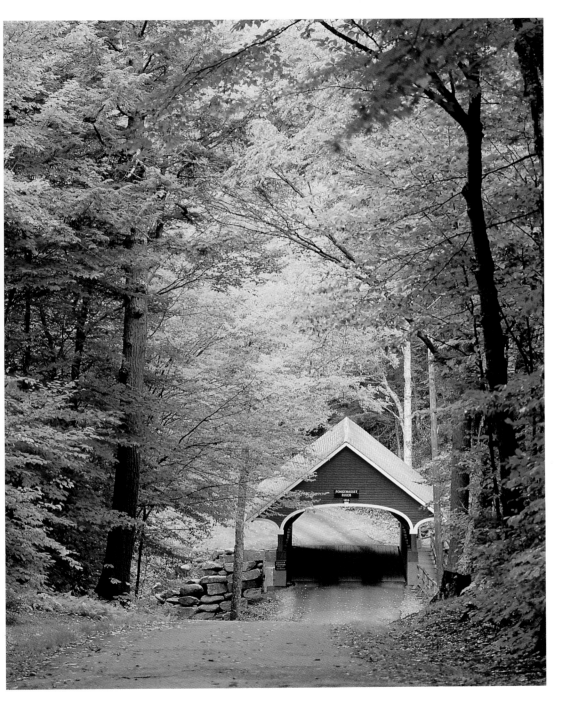

As well as serene landscapes such as this, Franconia Notch State Park has amazing formations such as the Flume, an 800-foot-high gorge, and Old Man of the Mountain, a granite cliff that resembles a man's profile.

OPPOSITE—
A covered bridge and the United Methodist Church paint a tranquil fall scene in Stark, home to just 500 people.

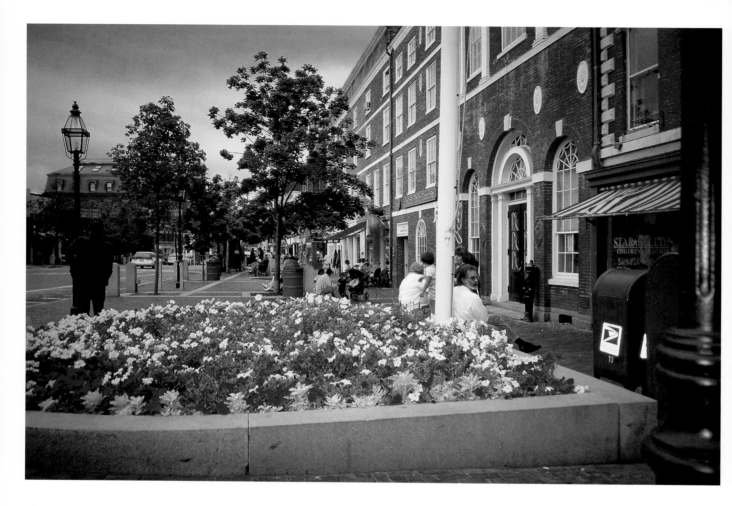

Shipbuilding has been an integral part of Portsmouth's history since the settlement's founding in 1623. The city retains picturesque streets and brick buildings from centuries ago.

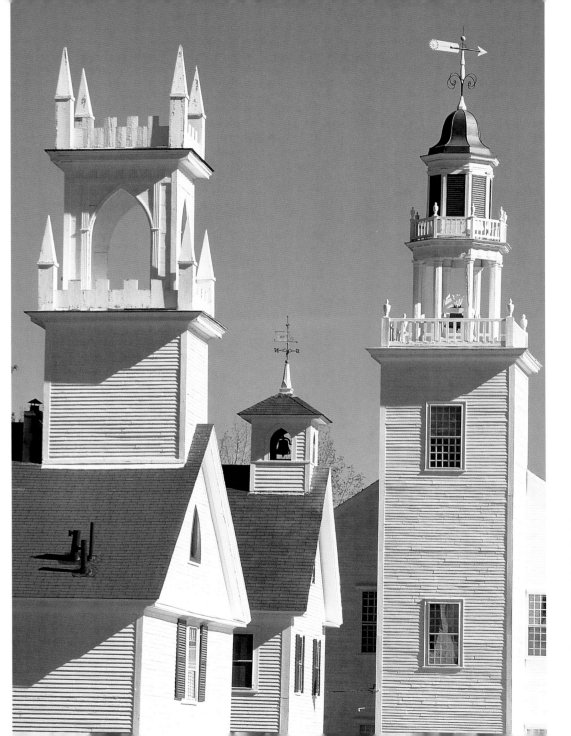

New Hampshire is only 90 miles across at its widest point. The forests that cover 80 percent of the state are interspersed with numerous small towns and coastal villages.

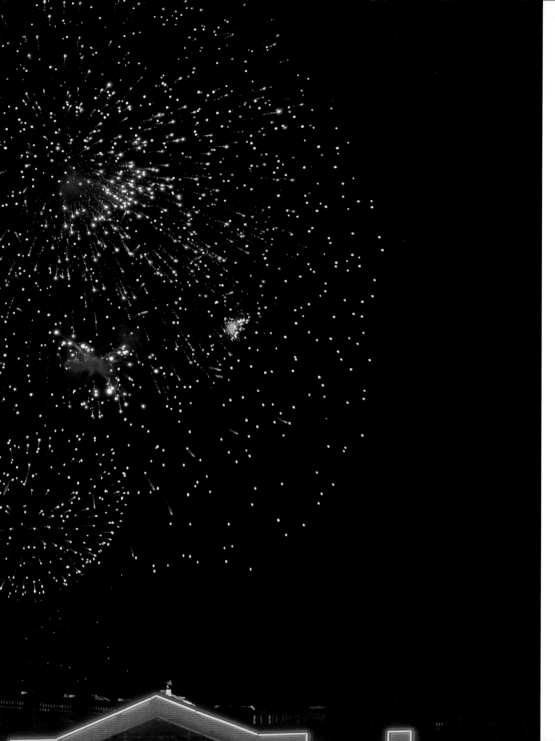

The state capitol
in Concord was
completed in 1819,
built of granite quar-
ried by prisoners of
the New Hampshire
State Prison. The
State House still
sits in the building's
original chambers.

In 1808, Concord was named New Hampshire's state capital, partly because of its central location. The arrival of the railway in 1842 assured the city's continued prosperity.

From native artifacts to a vintage Concord Coach—a famous and apparently technologically perfect coach invented here in the 19th century—Concord's Museum of New Hampshire History commemorates all ages of the state's past.

Founded in the late 18th century, the small town of Harrisville grew around the local woolen mill and is the only surviving industry town from that time still in its original form. Harrisville was declared a National Historic Landmark in 1977.

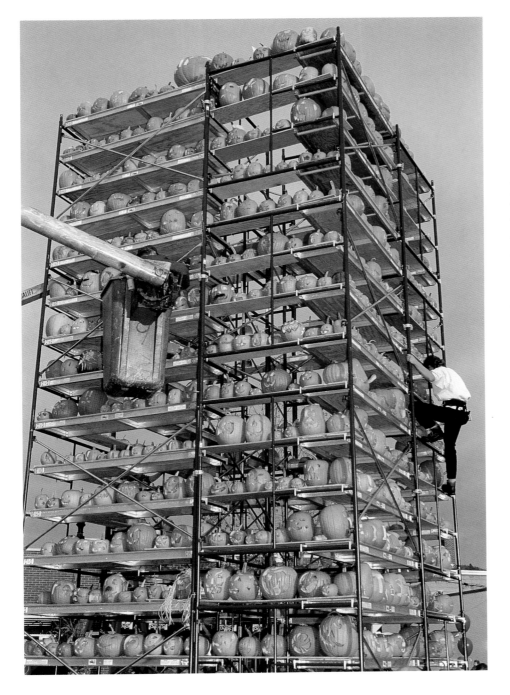

Keene is listed in the Guinness World Records for having the most jack-o'-lanterns in one place at one time. Every year, during the annual pumpkin festival, over 25,000 pumpkins are lit in the town's Central Square. Keene first broke the record in 1992, and each year attempts to improve on its previous showing.

OPPOSITE—
Azaleas adorn the village green in Keene. Among the city's other attractions are the widest main street in the nation and the lively surroundings of Keene State College.

Along with the tower of pumpkins, Halloween events in Keene include hay rides, fire engine rides, and trick-or-treating. One year, a beau in the holiday spirit carved his proposal into pumpkins during the festival.

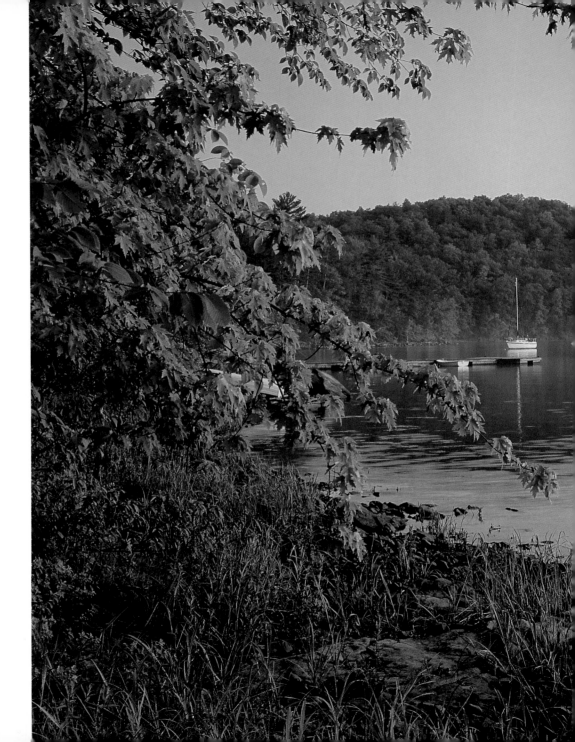

Stretching across the Canadian border into Quebec, Lake Champlain is the sixth-largest lake in the United States. The area is one of Vermont's most popular boating and fishing destinations.

From cross-country skiing in the surrounding hills and downhill skiing on Mount Mansfield to summer cycling and hiking, the town of Stowe is a mecca for outdoor enthusiasts.

At 4,383 feet high, Mount Mansfield soars above Vermont. A gondola whisks visitors to the summit, where they can take in a panoramic view of the region.

When the von Trapp family of *The Sound of Music* fame escaped Austria, they settled in Stowe, choosing the area partly because the local mountains reminded them of the Alps. The family established a lodge and singing camp nearby.

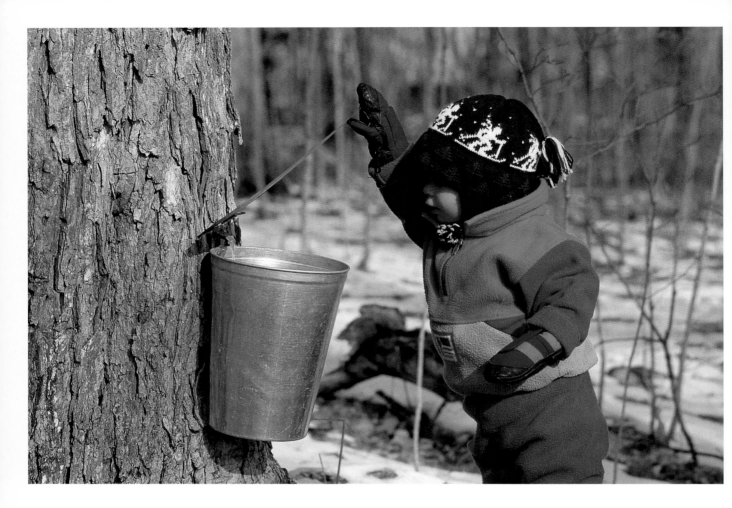

Traditionally, when making maple syrup, trees are tapped to allow sap to run into metal buckets. The buckets are then carried to the sugarhouse where the sap is boiled. Vermont produces close to a million gallons of maple syrup each spring.

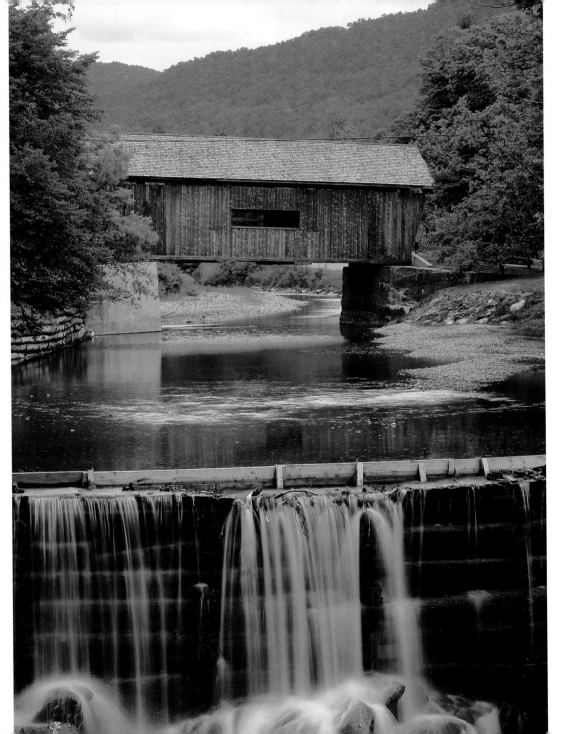

Set in the midst of Vermont's ski region, the rural beauty of Warren, complete with a covered bridge across the rushing Mad River, offers a quiet retreat to both visitors and residents.

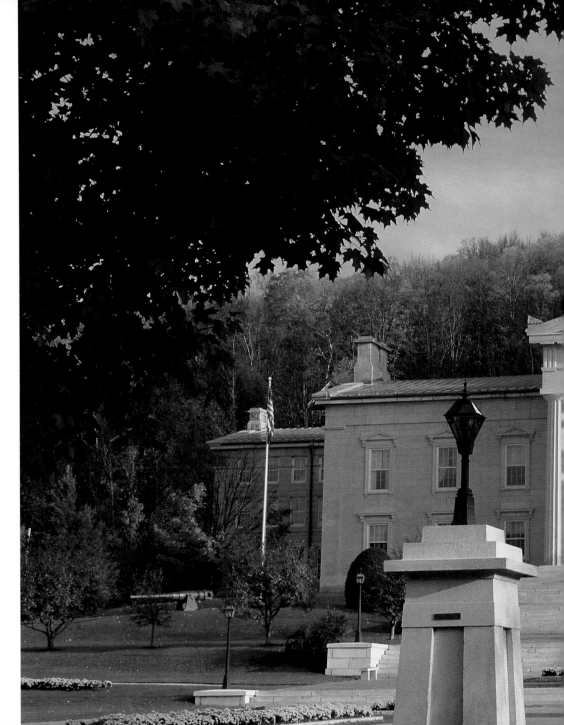

The sparkling dome of Vermont's state capitol dominates Montpelier, a town of fewer than 10,000 people. Built of local granite, the capitol was completed in 1859.

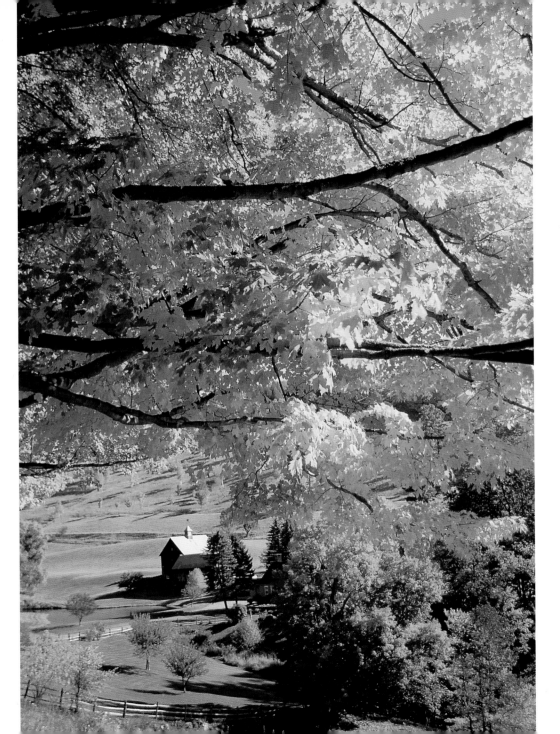

The church bells in Woodstock have a rare claim to fame—they were cast by New England legend Paul Revere. The Rockefellers have been residents of this region for more than a century.

OPPOSITE—
The tiny village of Peacham is believed to have been named after character Polly Peacham in John Gay's *The Beggar's Opera.* The actress who played the role in 18th-century Britain, Lavinia Fenton, married a duke and her real-life romance story was followed devotedly in Britain and America.

Christmas gifts and decorations adorn the shop windows of
Newburyport. Once a prosperous port, this charming town
is known for the heritage mansions of Victorian sea captains.
Many homes are complete with widow's walks, where sailors'
wives could watch for the return of their husbands' ships.

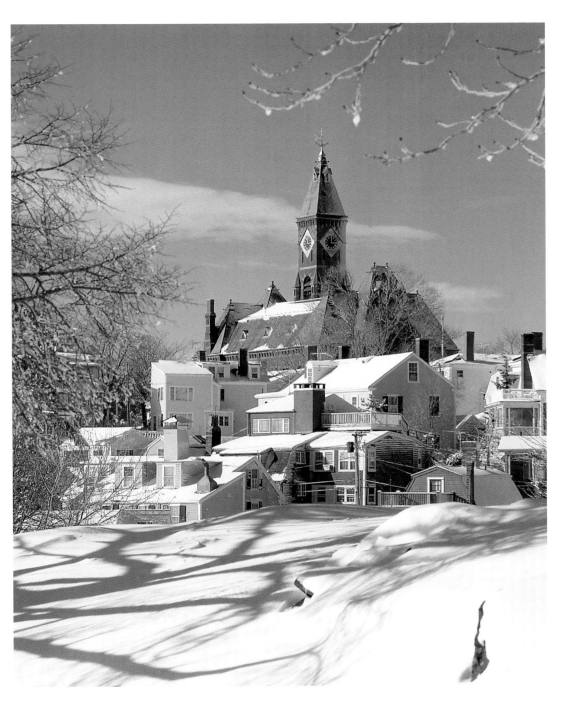

In 1760, Marblehead was the sixth-largest city in the American colonies. Abbot Hall, visible here amidst the town's historic district, houses Archibald M. Willard's famous painting *The Spirit of '76*.

Salem—best known as "Witch City"—has more to its history than the infamous witch trials. The House of Seven Gables, pictured here, was the inspiration. for 19th-century resident Nathaniel Hawthorne's book of the same name.

Now a national historic landmark, Walden Pond was the home of Henry David Thoreau from 1845 to 1847. The area inspired his book *Walden*, which helped spark the environmental conservation movement.

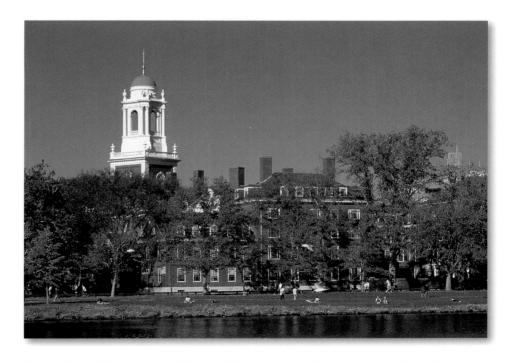

More than 350 years old, Harvard University in Cambridge was founded only 16 years after the Pilgrims arrived at Plymouth. More than 18,000 students study here under 2,000 faculty members.

The Head of the Charles Regatta is held each October in Cambridge on the Charles River. The largest two-day rowing event in the world, it draws 5,500 participants. Winners claim the title "Head of the Charles."

The State House in Boston soars over centuries of history. Among other major events, this city was the site of the 1773 Boston Tea Party, when American colonists boarded British ships and dumped more than 300 chests of tea overboard to protest high taxes on the beverage.

Boston is home to many "firsts." Ether was invented at Massachusetts General Hospital in 1846. Alexander Graham Bell invented the telephone here in 1876, and the world's first fire alarm was installed in Boston.

When the city of Boston planned to revamp the streets of Beacon Hill in the 1940s, local women staged a sit-in so that the characteristic brick sidewalks would be preserved.

In 1775, Paul Revere rode from Boston to Lexington, warning of an impending British attack. His journey was immortalized in Henry Wadsworth Longfellow's poem *Paul Revere's Ride.* Today, visitors can take a self-guided tour of the silver-smith's home.

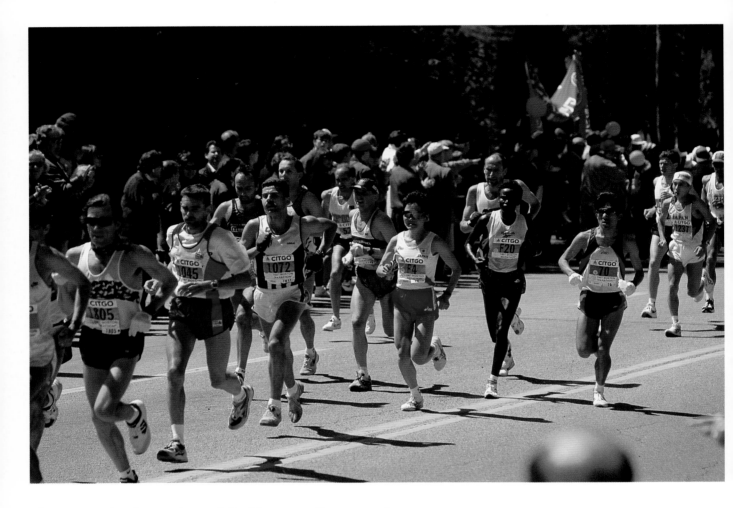

The Boston Marathon is the world's oldest annually contested marathon. Each year, approximately 20,000 people cross the finish line in front of the Boston Public Library.

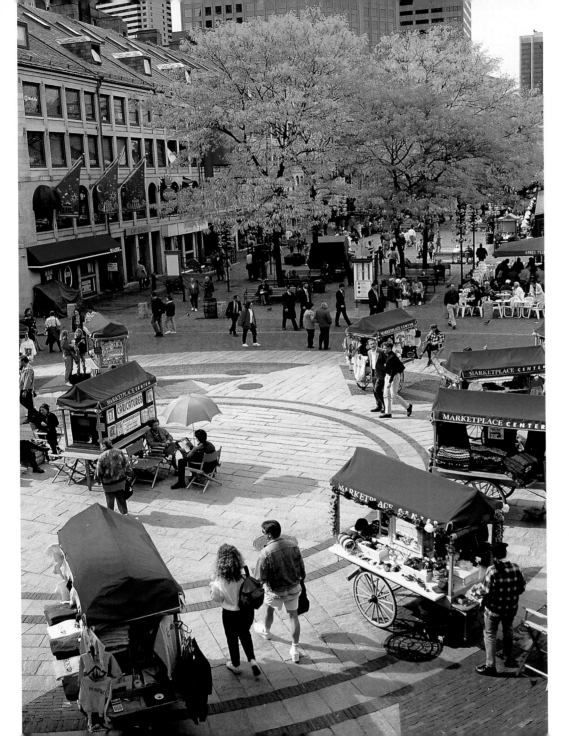

Pushcarts offer art, crafts, and giftware to passersby. The colorful vendors are part of Faneuil Hall Marketplace, a complex of galleries, restaurants, and retail stores.

Cranberries are indigenous to New England and have been cultivated since the mid-19th century. Cranberries are Massachusetts' most important agricultural product and workers harvest more than 12,000 acres each year.

Best known for celebrating the first Thanksgiving, the Pilgrims arrived in present-day Massachusetts in 1620. Just over 100 passengers made the voyage on the *Mayflower*, but only half survived the first New England winter.

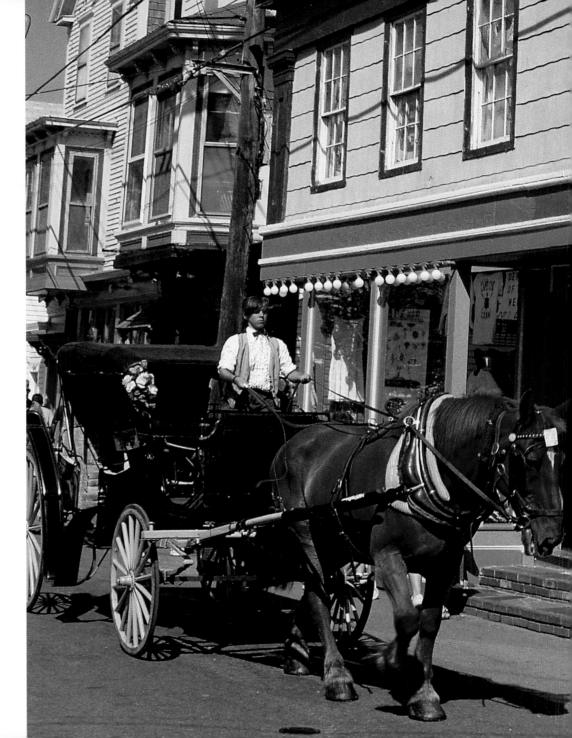

In 1620, the
Pilgrims anchored
in Provincetown's
harbor, remaining for
more than a month
before moving on
to Plymouth. Today,
Provincetown is best
known for its thriving
arts community,
and galleries line
the busy streets.

Built in 1663,
Brewster Mill is
still grinding corn,
mostly for tourists
as a souvenir of
Cape Cod.

According to local legend, British explorer Bartholomew Gosnold discovered Martha's Vineyard in the 1600s. He named it for his daughter Martha and for the abundant grapes he found growing wild on the island.

Cape Cod National Seashore encompasses 43,557 acres, including a pristine 40-mile stretch of shoreline. About 5 million people visit the area each year.

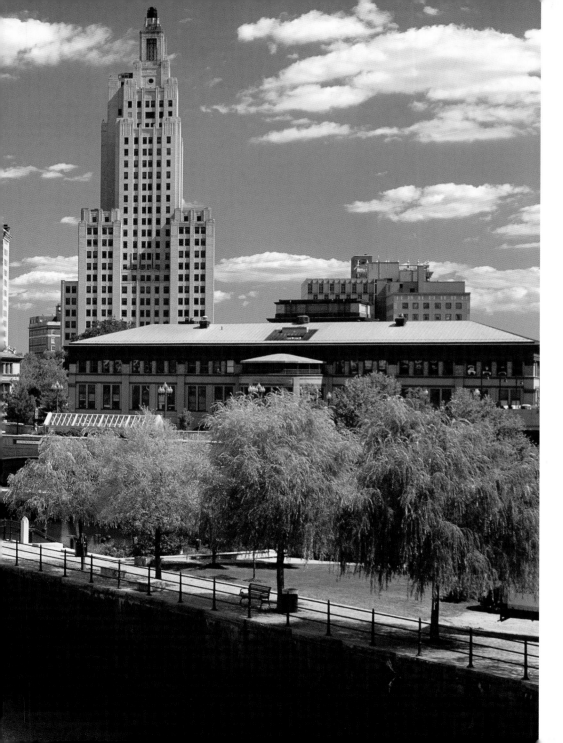

Completed in 1994, Waterplace Park and Riverwalk is a 400-acre park in the middle of Providence's downtown core. A series of cobblestone walkways and Venice-inspired bridges form a public space where visual and performance art are prominent. WaterFire, a work of art centered around 100 bonfires, draws crowds to the park throughout the summer.

The Providence
Preservation Society
helps care for the
hundreds of historic
homes in the city.
Many privately owned
buildings are opened
to the public several
times a year for tours.

Providence's Brown University was established in 1764. The school is noted for its unique undergraduate curriculum, designed by former president Francis Wayland so that every student "might study what he chose, all that he chose, and nothing but what he chose."

Designed in 1891, Rhode Island's state capitol boasts one of the world's four self-supported domes. The other three adorn St. Peter's Basilica, the Taj Mahal, and the Minnesota state capitol.

A town of just over 20,000 people for most of the year, Bristol draws 10 times that many revelers every Fourth of July. Fireworks and the oldest parade in the nation are part of the festivities.

OPPOSITE—
One of 12 extravagant mansions under the care of the Preservation Society of Newport County, Marble House was designed by Richard Morris Hunt and built in 1892 for William K. Vanderbilt.

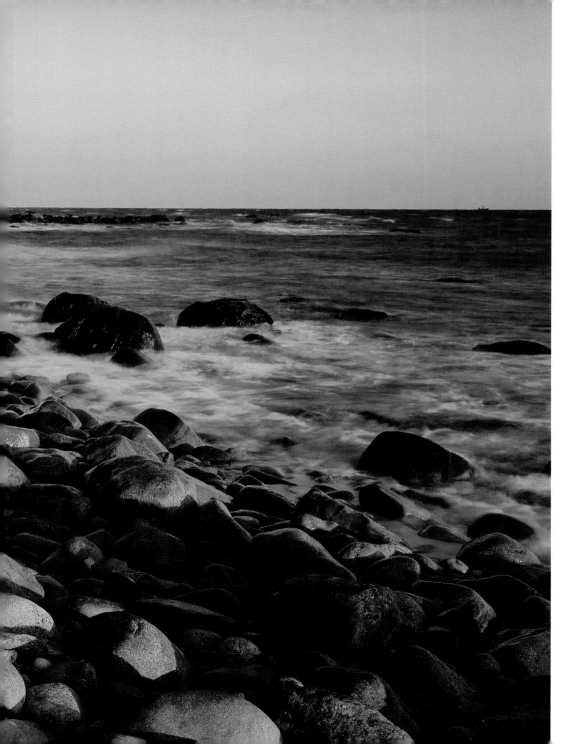

The 200-foot-high Mohegan Bluffs greet visitors to Block Island, 13 miles off Rhode Island's coast. The island manages to balance the charming tourist destination of Old Harbor with the conservation of pristine wetlands, home to more than 150 bird species.

Charlestown's four miles of beaches attract scores of swimmers and boaters. Some of the shoreline, along with Rhode Island's largest saltwater marsh, is protected by the nearby Ninigret National Wildlife Refuge.

Wandering through the Mystic Seaport Museum is like traveling back in time. Along with about 300 vessels, this lively attraction includes a children's museum and the traditional shops of a 19th-century village.

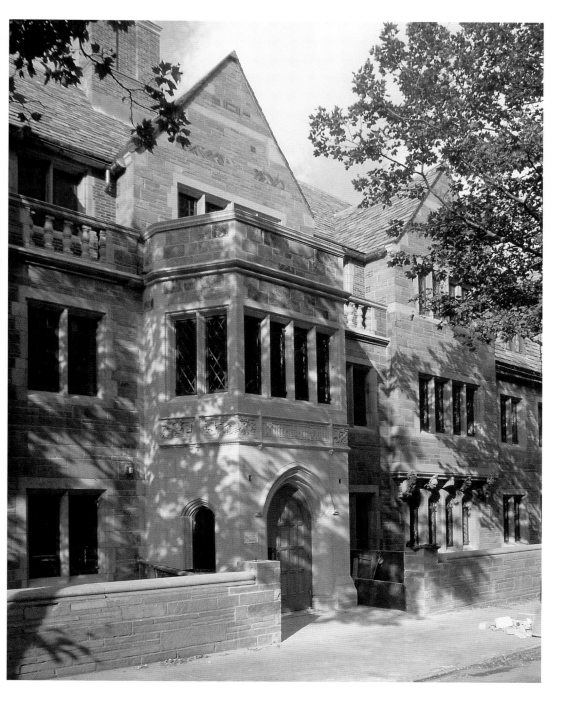

In 1718, trader and philanthropist Elihu Yale endowed his fortune on the school which bears his name. More than 10,000 students attend classes on the 200-acre New Haven campus.

OPPOSITE—
Steeples of three churches grace New Haven Green. The 16-acre square was set aside by village elders in the 1600s and remains the town center.

Chapman Falls
tumbles 60 feet into
a bubbling basin in
Devil's Hopyard State
Park in Connecticut.

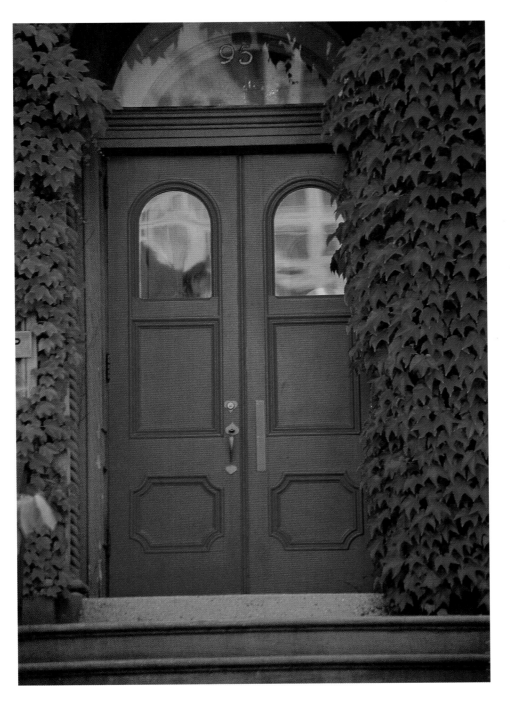

Ivy-covered buildings, such as this one, are a common sight in Hartford. Ivy on the exterior of a building can help to keep its interior cool.

OPPOSITE—
Hartford Riverfest is the city's annual Fourth of July celebration. The daylong event includes musical performances, displays, and children's activities, and ends with a large fireworks display over the Connecticut River.

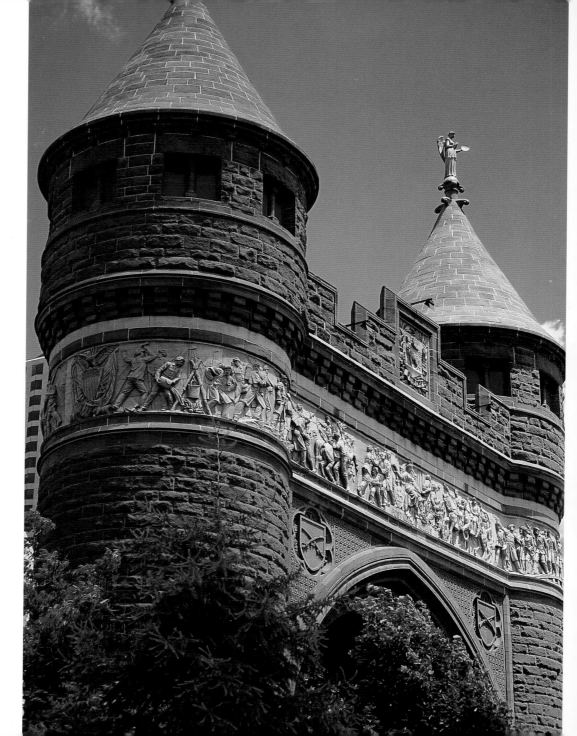

One hundred feet tall and 30 wide, the Soldiers and Sailors Memorial Arch honors those who fought in the Civil War. It stands in Hartford's famous Bushnell Park, which was designed by Frederick Law Olmsted.

OPPOSITE—
The country's oldest continuously operating ferry has linked Glastonbury—just 10 miles southeast of Hartford—with Rocky Hill since 1655.

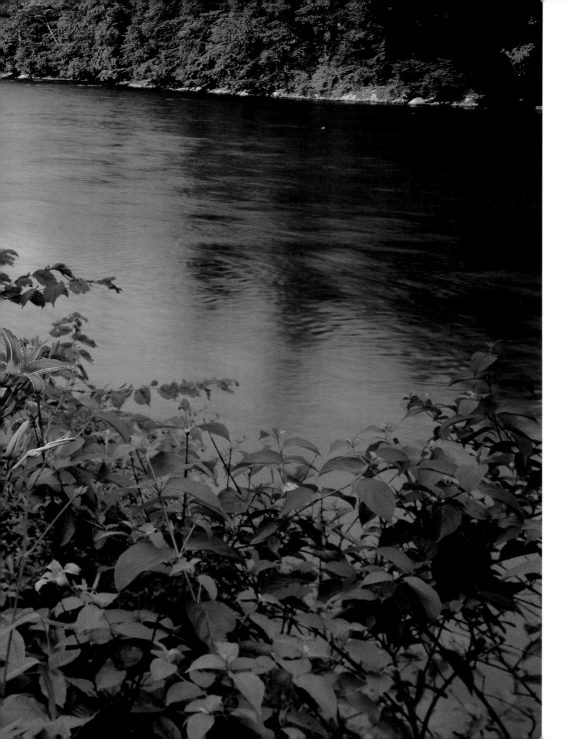

The Housatonic River, a favorite destination for anglers, runs through Bulls Bridge Nature Preserve. Local legend holds that George Washington's horse plunged into the river near here after slipping on a bridge.

Photo Credits